All interviews from

2016

Michael Kenna
Steve McCurry
Irene Kung
Longh Than
Josef Koudelka
Stuart Franklin
Sarah Moon
Frank Horvat
Massimo Vitali
Szymon Brodziak
John G. Morris

All interviews were conducted by Enrico Ratto and translated by Elisa Chisana Hoshi, unless otherwise stated.

Frank Horvat's interviews are from the book Entre Vues.

Monthly interviews with the best international photographers

Michael Kenna:
I look for silence as an escape from the background noise of the world

Michael Kenna, is it true that when you were young you wanted to study to become a Catholic priest?

I did indeed attend a junior seminary school with the intention to become a Catholic priest! Perhaps it is best if I describe the journey in some detail. I was born and brought up in what might be described as a poor, working class family in Widnes, an industrial town near Liverpool in England. Childhood experiences obviously have a great influence on one's life, and as a boy, even though I had five older siblings, I was quite solitary, content for the most part with making up my own adventures and acting them out in the local parks and streets. I liked to wander in train stations and factories, on rugby grounds and canal tow-paths, and in empty churches and grave yards, all locations that I would later find interesting to photograph.

Locations that later became objects of your photography.

Even though I did not use a camera at the time, I suspect this period was ultimately more influential on my vision than the time I later spent in art and photography schools. During these young years I had been an altar boy at my local Catholic church of St Bede's and I really loved to be part of the great religious rituals of the church, assisting the priest at baptisms, funerals, weddings and the Latin mass. When I was almost eleven years old I went to a Catholic seminary boarding school at my own request, to study to become a priest. My experiences during the subsequent seven years I stayed, taught me important lessons about life. There were also many aspects of this religious upbringing that I believe strongly influenced my later photographic work, including discipline, silence, meditation and a sense that something can be unseen, yet still very present.

From a professional point of view, you left religion to embrace art.

The education was excellent, but the "career guidance" was not very strong. In my teen years I decided that I didn't want to follow a religious life and had to decide what I did want to do. Fortunately, I seemed to be good at drawing and painting, so, following these interests, I went on to study at the Banbury School of Art in Oxfordshire with an intention to have a career in the arts. This is where painting and photography appeared as specific options amongst many others. I felt that the chances of supporting myself as a painter in England were very low and I knew that I had to fend for myself, so I decided to specialize in photography at the London College of Printing.

Is this when you started to shoot landscapes?

Essentially, I was trained to be a commercial photographer. I learnt about photojournalism, fashion photography, sports photography, still-live photography, architectural photography, all sorts of photography with many different cameras. When I graduated, I was competent enough to be able to survive in a competitive commercial photography world. This is what I initially did. Running parallel to this, I was also consistently photographing the landscape, which was my necessary means of self expression. I had no idea at the time that I could and would eventually make a living in this latter area.

For over thirty years you have shot many different places of earth and chased what we could define as slow photography. At what point do you realize that you have finally found the right spot to put the tripod of your Hasselblad?

When I photograph I look for some sort of resonance, connection, spark of recognition. Usually, I do not make any elaborate preparation before I go to a location. Essentially I walk, explore and photograph. I never know whether I will be in a place for minutes, hours or days. Approaching subject matter to photograph is for me a bit like meeting a person and beginning a conversation. How does one know ahead of time where that dialogue will lead, what the subject matter will be, how intimate it will become, how long the potential relationship will last? Feelings can be complicated, confused and mixed.

Are you still surprised by the way that reality reveals itself?

I try not to jump to immediate conclusions for there have been many occasions when interesting images have appeared from what I had considered uninteresting places. The reverse has been equally true and relevant. One needs to fully accept that surprises sometimes happen and control over outcome is not always necessary or even desirable. Of course, there are the exceptional moments when I feel a tingle of recognition and my hair seems to stand up. Exquisite moments when the equation of light, subject matter, point of view and technical excellence all combine to produce what I might think of at the time as a masterpiece. This is a rare occurrence in my experience, and the final image from such magical serendipity often falls short of my expectations. Hence, the mistrust I have in my own ability to predict exactly how something will come out. I prefer Garry Winogrand's philosophy of photographing to see how something looks photographed!

What your pictures makes us feel, through their landscapes and black and white imagery, is the silence.

In my work I try to present an oasis of quiet calm and solitude that viewers of the final image can enter into. At the beginning of my photographic explorations I preferred to photograph in the early morning because there were fewer people around, and little or no "chatter" in the air. Morning light is often soft and diffused. It can reduce a cluttered background to graduated layers of two dimensional tone. I still prefer the dawn hours more than any other time of the day or night, but now I photograph at all hours, day and night. Our world is fast paced, colorful, full of distractions and all too often, extremely loud! I try to create order from chaos, and often seek silence as an escape from the world's constant background noise.

At the end of the 70's you moved from England to Ruth Bernhard's studio in San Francisco to dedicate yourself to photographic printing.

I was very fortunate to meet Ruth Bernhard in 1978. She had just signed an exclusive contract with The Stephen White Gallery in Los Angeles, in which she agreed to make many prints over a period of two years. Unfortunately for her, she had recently suffered some carbon monoxide poisoning and did not feel able to make these prints. I had also just begun to be represented by the same gallery and Stephen kindly asked me if I would be interested to help Ruth. It was a wonderful opportunity it for me.

This is a background of knowledge that you carry with you every day.

My ten years of working with Ruth Bernhard were priceless. I cannot emphasize enough her influence on both my life and work. Before working with Ruth, I thought that I was a good photographic printer based on my previous experience. I had printed my own work and that of a number of other photographers, both in colour and black and white. However, Ruth gave me new insights into the process. Her basic starting point was that the negative was a starting point! She would radically transform an initial straight print into a Ruth Bernhard print. This might involve tilting the easel to achieve a different perspective, softening the focus to create an evenness of tone, making masks to burn and dodge, using different chemicals to change the contrast or color of the image, etc. She essentially refused to believe that the impossible wasn't possible, and she taught me that there were no rules that couldn't be broken. This made for many very late nights in her darkroom!

Once again, you point out the importance of having great teachers.

Ruth often said that she regarded her role of teacher to be far more important than her role of photographer. At the time, I was a young photographer trying to navigate in the extremely puzzling world of art galleries, publishers and commercial agents. Ruth was a guiding light for me. "Today is the day" was her mantra, and her determination to live in the present, to appreciate every moment, to always say yes to life, has left an indelible impression on me. I remain in debt to her kindness and wisdom.

Do you think that coming from an industrial zone in England had an influence on your way of looking at a landscape?

I feel that growing up in Widnes, an industrial town, has been highly influential in my work. I have photographed industry quite extensively throughout my career, including the cotton and wool mills in Lancashire and Yorkshire, power stations in the Midlands and Scotland, the Rouge Steel plant in Detroit, Michigan, USA, and lace factories in Calais, France. Industry is very much a part of our landscape and I have always felt drawn to photograph it.

Industry is the theme of your upcoming book that will be published next autumn.

Yes, perhaps this is a good time to announce that my next book to be published by Prestel this Autumn will be titled Rouge. It will be based on the the work that I did in the nineties at the Ford Motor Plant in Dearborn, Michigan.
The paintings and photographs of Charles Sheeler were the primary influences for this Rouge project. At the time, I was represented close to Detroit by the Halsted Gallery and they were able to introduce me to a retired Ford employee, Lee Kollins, who kindly gave me a tour of the Rouge facilities. I remember that I was at first less than impressed and did not feel that there was much potential for photographic imagery. However, as often happens, upon processing the film and seeing the results, I immediately realized how mistaken I had been. I returned to photograph the Rouge very soon thereafter and continued to photograph over the next three years, during the day and at night. These negatives are the basis for the upcoming book.

Have you always shot landscapes in black and white?

As a student, I experimented with colour. As a young photographer I worked as a colour printer. As a professional, I have photographed in colour for a number of commercial projects and a few personal. However, it is ultimately not my preferred palette. I feel that black and white photographs are generally quieter and more mysterious than those made in colour. For me, the subtlety of black and white inspires the imagination of the individual viewer to complete the picture in their mind's eye. It doesn't attempt to compete with the outside world. I believe it is calmer and more gentle than colour, and persists longer in our visual memory. After all, we see in colour all the time. Black and white is therefore immediately an interpretation of the world rather than a copy of what we see.

As a photographer, you only work in analog and print using your own dark room.

At this point, I am still 100% analog. I use film cameras and insist on making all prints myself in my own traditional wet darkroom. Having said that, I believe that every photographer, every artist, should choose materials and equipment based on their own personal vision. I don't believe that analog is better than digital, or the reverse for that matter. They are just different, and it is my personal preference and choice to remain with the traditional silver process. I don't need or desire instant gratification in photography and it is the long, slow journey to the final print that captivates me. I still prefer the limitations, imperfections and unpredictability of the silver based analog world. Having worked with silver materials and film cameras for over forty years, both commercially and in my own fine art work, I now find it a little out of character to fully embrace the digital medium even though I have experimented a little with it. It is true that the whole photographic process has been made much easier, faster, cleaner and more accessible to people by digital innovations, and that's a very good thing. It doesn't mean that all photographers need to follow this tidal wave. I think that while analog materials and chemicals are still being manufactured, I will probably stay away from digital. But, who knows what the future might bring.

Why do you choose to print your wide landscapes in such an intimate, small format?

I've experimented with bigger prints a number of times on various projects, but, for most of my work I prefer the more intimate, smaller, precious print. Our eyes see about 35 degrees in focus so we naturally approach artwork from a certain distance. I prefer viewers to be about ten inches from my prints, which becomes a very intimate one-on-on viewing engagement. I choose my print size accordingly. Also, I have printed this way since the seventies Older prints get along fine being exhibited next to recent prints and my work has become one large, quite happy family.

Let's talk about solitude, another key element of your photography. A great Italian author once said that solitude is important because it allows someone to get in touch with their surroundings, which are not only made up of human beings.

I agree with the musician and prefer to be able to listen to my surroundings when working seriously. I think the act of photographing is quite similar to that of having a conversation. If I photograph a tree, for example, I consciously ask permission from the tree to make a portrait, then we have a conversation. It is a shared experience and the resulting image is a collaboration. Quite simply, I find it easier to concentrate when there are no other people around to distract me.

Is that why you like solitude?

On a more philosophical level, we arrive in this world alone and we leave it alone. I believe it is incredibly important to be comfortable with our own solitude. Much of my work is about the presence of absence. I rarely have people in my photographs as I want the viewer to imagine being there alone in these empty spaces. Often, I use the analogy of the performing arts, theatre for example. I prefer to photograph the stage before the actors appear or after they have left, when there is a strong atmosphere of anticipation. In these moments we have to use our individual imagination to create a personal story. When the actors appear on stage we tend to listen to and follow their story. I like to think of my images as invitations to enter into quiet, empty spaces and experience solitude. In our everyday crowded, chaotic world sometimes this is not so easy to do. It can also be quite uncomfortable. However, I believe it is incredibly important to allow our minds the time and space to freely roam and explore.

I read that you like running; and that just as long runs allow you to work on the body, long photography exposures allow you to work on the mind.

I do like to run and have just completed my 55th 26.2 mile marathon. For me, it is a form of meditation and keeps me in decent physical condition, which is very important for a landscape photographer who often has to walk a long way with a heavy backpack and tripod! Another beneficial side effect of long distance running is the opportunity to freely use our imagination. During a long run, I have often unconsciously thought of creative solutions to miscellaneous problems. On a more logistical level, I have discovered many good locations while running which I have returned to photograph later.

There is an American association called The Long Now Foundation, which invites us to focus on a life horizon of more than ten thousand years, instead of the usual seventy or eighty years of our lives. This would allow us to get a different perspective on what we actually think and produce. If you close your eyes and think of your daily life, what time horizon do you see?

I once had a dream that I was a giant chestnut tree. It seemed that as I grew, centuries came and went. I looked down from where I stood and observed generations of people, individuals and families, going about their lives. Our ongoing human stories – often viewed through the subjective prisms of drama, comedy or tragedy – seemed to take on a whole different light when viewed from this new perspective. I think that when I woke up, I was a changed person. My attitude towards time was profoundly affected and my respect for these beautiful trees, these sentinels of experience, was dramatically increased.

But Ruth Bernhard taught you to live in the present, living our life, not that of the chestnut tree.

Yes, I feel that it is ultimately most important to think about the present. I am constantly aware that time is passing, even accelerating. I want to make the most of whatever time I have in this life.
I really don't want to waste a second. It is beyond my comprehension that I will be 63 years old in November! Where did all those years go to? Life is precious and fleeting. I will certainly look ahead to the future, even though it may never arrive, and I will occasionally glance back at the past, even though there is nothing about it that I can change, but the present is what concerns me the most.

Steve McCurry:
go deep, wait for things to happen

Steve McCurry, you work on many projects, you have exhibitions in many places in the world simultaneously and also write many books. I guess that aside from a great staff, you also have many deep values that you wish to share…

I think the most important thing in life is to communicate your joy. It's important to live your life in the direction that you feel will lead you to fulfill your dreams and values, everything that is meaningful to you. Do things that you consider important in a way that when you look back you see something that makes sense, just like in a puzzle.

What does a book like "The stories behind the photographs" add to your photos?

I think that it gives a whole new dimension and another side to my work. I think that meeting the public in person, presenting the book, adds a more spontaneous approach than pictures seen in a magazine or an exhibition could ever have on their own. It's a fundamental way to show my personality.

Books, exhibitions, works for magazines: in which of those are you able to better express your work?

It's difficult to say. It's like in the human body, which part is more important than another? A leg, an arm, a face… everything is equally important in my job, and I can't separate all the elements from each other.

Ferdinando Scianna says that photos have little or nothing to

do with paintings, that photos are not canvases but pieces of literature. What do you think about that?

There are many different elements in a photo. First of all, a photo certainty tells a story, it's a narration of a person's behavior in his own world. That's why I partly agree with Scianna, also because he shoots in black and white. Me, however, I shoot predominantly in color, and there are aspects in color – for example the way colors work together – that lead people to compare them to a painting. People often don't know the story behind a photo, just like they experience with a painting: what they see is all they know. I think that photography is a medium that serves the purpose of telling a story in the most immediate and universal way possible.

What do you need to tell the public a story: a single shot or a whole reportage?

I hope to be able to communicate a story through a photo. Reportages drag you deeply inside the story, but a story can definitely be told through a single shot. Each and every photo tells different aspects of a story: if you put them together they will complement each other.

This year's World Press Photo was won by John Stanmeyer's shot, which shows two of the pillars of this age that we are living in: communication and travel. Are those the pillars of your life too?

They certainly are. There is no doubt whatsoever, communication and travel are the bases of my life. Nine out of twelve months of the year I am traveling, and I am taking pictures the whole time.

You are part of a generation that traveled to find stories. Traveling nowadays is much more simple and accessible. Is it still necessary to travel far from home to take pictures or can we find depth next to our home, in our family or just down our street?

Today it's certainly possible to tell powerful stories close to home. I think that it all boils down to what you want to experience in your life. I think that every photographer chooses what to explore at different times in his life, and it's such a personal choice. Taking pictures of your own family, neighbours, road and city is a completely respectable choice. Besides, sometimes the events come close to you. I myself reported on 9/11 in New York, that was something happening close to me in places that I knew very well.

Are there times when you are not intrigued by a place, to the point where you say there is nothing around?

Sure, it happens all the time. The challenge is to continuously go deep, devote time to do research, waiting for things to happen while observing a place for a longtime.

When you arrive somewhere, what do you wait for before you shoot?

I look for the right moment, the right light; I try to work out a good photo. All this requires experience, ability, talent and sense, the capacity to recognize a strong situation or a unique face. Perception is crucial with people. I don't study much before starting a project. I go there and I discover, I think it's much more amusing to stay fresh towards the places that I'm about to visit. Having just a basic idea, to be free to move around with a fresh head.

If you look back on your archive, do you think that your story has evolved or that your projects change from time to time?

I think that there is continuity and all my works are connected. I have always worked in an area between Afghanistan, Cambodia, India, Tibet and Sri Lanka, where everything has a very particular origin. I believe in people that can charm us, in humanity, in relations between people and their habitat. That's what interests me.

Your first photos where in black and white, why did you then start shooting in color?

At a certain point I thought that it was more logical to use color, from the eighties onward a color picture probably makes more sense. The world is in color, and colors convey much more information.

How do you live with an icon, with the world saying: "Steve McCurry, the one who took the picture of the Afghan girl?"

Actually, I don't think that people only know me for that photo. There are, however, a lot of people that haven't studied music and know Beethoven, just like many people that are not interested in photography know that picture, the Afghan Girl. It's like that, and that's fine with me.

Irene Kung:
rational thinking can mislead us, our feelings do not

Irene Kung, your latest project is dedicated to trees, like the title suggests. What brought you to the idea of the Trees book and exposition?

Trees, especially fruit ones, symbolize productivity, health and fertility: in this time of economic crisis and difficulty, they embody a positive and universal image.

"Stopping to see, feel, think and dream" is the same approach that you adopted for your previous work The Invisible City. Is Trees an ideal continuation of that project, or does it represent more of a disruption?

There is no disruption between the two projects: in their own way, they both depict an element becoming part of an imaginary whole.

What does the word "essential" mean to you?

Essential means to bring the subject back to what I was feeling when shooting it. It means to erase any noise and show that tree or monument exactly the way I was feeling them.

Did your background in advertising and graphic design help you simplify and work on the essential?

It did. In graphic design it is vital to produce a clear message that everybody can understand. I learned how to simplify when I was painting. Picasso once said, "Perfection is achieved, not when there is nothing more to add, but when there is nothing left to take away."

All the captions in Trees are not about the places, but about the species of each tree. Once again, your pictures can't be confined to a place. Does photography take us in a different direction, a place that doesn't belong to a map?

This is true for my photography. The trees in this project don't belong to any specific place: the focus is on the many facets of their essence without losing their individuality as a lemon, olive or fig tree. It's not important to know where they are, but which emotions they convey.

You photographed monuments and even trees that others have shot before. So does it still make sense to say, "I photograph what interests me, I photograph my tree?"

I believe an artist should give the public what it lacks, and so the job of a contemporary artist is to allow people to dream through a positive and intimate message. When I choose my subject to shoot I try to ignite my emotions through them, while trying to reach the souls of whoever is looking at my pictures.

The work on trees inspires more silence than the work on buildings, don't you think?

Maybe it is because, even if in my photos the buildings appear submerged in the dark, we tend to imagine them in the middle of a city, surrounded by cars, tourists and noise. It is easier to access our emotions while looking at a tree that we naturally associate with a wood, with nature. Also, the building would not exist without humanity, unlike the trees.

Let's now talk about image manipulation. Frank Horvat, a great author and digital pioneer, told us that for him the postproduction is an opportunity not to correct per se, but to get what originally interested him when he was taking that picture. Do you recognize yourself in that?

Yes, absolutely. Like I said, I try to bring the subject back to exactly what I was feeling when shooting it. The postproduction helps me in that matter.

Your prints reignite the old debate about photography and painting. Do you thing about painting when you shoot or work on a picture?

Sure. I started as a painter and for me the camera is merely a tool to create images. When I work on photography I concentrate on the light with a very pictorial approach.

At what point do you stop shooting and furthermore, when do you stop working on an image?

When I'm satisfied with what I feel. It happens instantly with some pictures, but it can take months or even years with some others.

The strictness, the rules and guidelines of your projects are very evident. Have you ever feel limited by your own rules?

Having worked so much on monuments I felt the need to change, so I started the project Trees. Protecting the passion I feel towards my work is very important to me, I would not hesitate to find new challenges the day I feel that limitation.

Is dreaming just as important as real life?

Dreaming is a fundamental part of reality, it is intuition and irrationality. Rational thinking can mislead us, our feelings do not.

Long Thanh: photographing is like cooking with mastery

an interview by Elisa Chisana Hoshi

Long Thanh, you only take black and white pictures, why?

I believe in black and white and in the beauty of contrasts. For me, a better way to depict reality just does not exist. Black and white is simply marvellous.

When did you start taking pictures?

I was 13. I learned everything from my uncle, just observing him working and snooping around the back room of his shop. He had two photography shops and I learned everything there, no schools.

You live in Nha Trang, a small resort town on the Vietnamese seaside, far away from the capital Hanoi and Ho Chi Minh City.

That's right. I was born here, and here I have always lived and worked. Nha Trang is my home. I love its nature and its relaxed lifestyle. My family wasn't wealthy, I was the eighth of eleven kids and I never went to photography school. My dad was Chinese, my mum was Vietnamese: she was beautiful. She had an exquisite and petite figure, just like my daughter. You will meet her, she lives in Saigon but today she's here! My other daughter lives in Saigon too and looks much more like me. They don't live with us. My wife and I live in this house that is now my workshop and which I love so much, I bought it from my uncle. It used to be his studio.

There's a gorgeous old Vespa parked outside, in front of the studio...

She is one of my favorites! I love vintage Vespa, there is another one here in the studio too, have you seen that one?

I sure did, it's gorgeous! You live surrounded by your pictures and your cameras, such an amazing atmosphere.

Yes. Each and every picture is a unique piece that I shot and printed. I love everything about photography. I love shooting and also developing, crafting the picture from A to Z. The problem is that here in Vietnam there is no photography material; we don't produce anything of that kind. I have to buy everything from abroad: paper from the UK, the film from America – I use Kodak film since forever – and the chemicals from Germany. It's getting more and more expensive; paper just went up in price. I'll think of something. Luckily I have many friends that give me a hand to find all the material I need. That's also the beauty of photography.

Do you always know when to shoot?

Before I shoot I need a particular feeling with my subject: every picture follows that particular feeling, an actual moment of complicity. Behind every picture there is an unrepeatable moment.

I truly love your picture of the kid jumping from one buffalo's back to another, through the river's stream. When did you shoot that one?

That was in 1999, in a countryside village not far from Nha Trang, among the rice fields. It was early in the morning and I was walking along the river, carrying my camera with me. The kid you see in the picture saw me and smiled. All of a sudden he started to have fun: he jumped in the river and started to hop from one buffalo's back to another, like they were river stones! He was having so much fun. And the funny thing is, the buffaloes did not seem very surprized at all… I bet he was doing that every day! Just incredible. I truly enjoyed taking that picture.

How about light?

Light is a crucial element, one of the most important ones in photography. I like soft light, the one that smoothly enlightens everything. That's my style. That's why I love shooting in the morning, just after dawn, and in the evening, right before sunset. I love that warm light, it's rather special.

How is it being a photographer in Vietnam?

Here in Vietnam there aren't proper photography schools. As I told you it's very difficult to get the material necessary to shoot analogue photography. For digital it's different, obviously. I often take part in photography competitions as jury, but I stopped participating with my own pictures. I'll tell you why.

I have to admit that I have my own ideas and certainly don't like some the trends of today's competitions. I'm not a fan of showing off and of the savage use of Photoshop. I admire some of my Vietnamese colleagues, and I'm always happy to work with them: especially Le Hong Ling and Ly Hoang Long. They are young and talented, they really believe in what they do.

Concerning Nick Hut, and his world famous Pulitzer-winning shot, I've got something to show you. Look at this picture: that's me with Kim Phuc, the girl of the original picture; I met her a few years ago in America. She told me some stories and really personal things about the picture and Nick Hut, some secrets that I cannot tell you. I made her a promise. (Author's note: he actually tells me some of these secrets.)

What do you consider an original picture?

It's a picture that comes after a lot of thinking and crafting. It's somehow like a good dish of spaghetti: it has to be cooked with mastery. You cut the veggies, you handpick all the ingredients and finish up by adding some virgin olive oil and Parmesan.

A picture retouched with Photoshop is like the same dish of spaghetti, but with mayonnaise and ketchup. It can be tasty, you might like it… but it's certainly not the same thing! They say that I'm old fashioned, but I'm not. I love new technology (Author's note: while we speak he keeps playing with his iPad). Only, I'm a bit of a purist in photography. The digital black and white is not even close to the film one. It's more of a monochrome.

You have an impressive collection of vintage cameras. Which one is your favourite?

I love all my vintage Leica but my favourite is this one. Wait, I'm going to fetch it for you, you really have to see it up close. It's a Hasselblad SWC. A Zweiss lens and a Swedish body... she is my Swedish girlfriend!

I understand that you are fascinated by Europe, that you like good wine and good food. Have you ever been to Italy?

No, not yet. But my pictures have twice. First in Rome, during the Festival dedicated to Vietnamese culture in 2007, then in Lecco in 2009, the Galleria Melesi did an exhibit about me.
I'd really love to come to Italy and shoot the beautiful chiaroscuro of its roads. Italy and its lifestyle, the beautiful clothes, the amazing cooking, it all fascinates me. I'd love to depict your country through my style: in black and white!

Josef Koudelka:
a good photo is a miracle

an interview by Frank Horvat

First interview, January 1987

You ask if I have made good use of my vision. I believe I have used it too little. Photographers like Henri (Cartier-Bresson) always have a camera with them and are looking all the time. I don't know how to do that. Right now, for example, I am not looking, my mind is occupied by words.

What do you mean by "I am not looking"?

I am not looking with the idea to make a photograph.

How are you looking?

I am seeing only a few of things around me. Only those that I want to see.

But to see what you want to see, you have to look. And to choose..

It seems to me that, to see "photographically", I have to prepare myself in advance. Possibly for a long time. For instance it would be difficult for me, on my way out from here, to make photos of Paris. To see, I would have to go to another city, say to New York, live in a hotel room by myself and start walking through the streets, at first without a camera. And little by little I would begin to see. In the same way, I wouldn't know how to make a portrait of a woman, just off the hip. I would have to think about her, to imagine her. She would have to prepare herself or to be prepared with someone's help. And even then,

when I would eventually be facing her, with my camera, I might not feel ready. It could take me two or three hours to understand her, little by little, through the viewfinder.

Perhaps because you want to understand. Me, I do not try to understand. For me, the most beautiful thing is to wake up, to go out, and to look. At everything. Without anyone telling me "You should look at this or that." I look at everything and I try to find what interests me, because when I set out, I don't yet know what will interest me. Sometimes I photograph things that others would find stupid, but with which I can play around. Henri as well says that before meeting a person, or seeing a country, he has to prepare himself. Not me, I try to react to what comes up. Afterwards, I may come back to it, perhaps every year, ten years in a row, and I will end by understanding.

You prepare yourself in your way. I imagine that when you find a subject that interests you, your photo is, in a way, already prepared within you. As if you had set up a place into which it fits.

What's "my photo"?

Your photos often are recognizable, which is to say that they have something in common. Maybe the space between the figures, and the tensions within that space.

I don't know. But I interrupted you, you were speaking about yourself.

If I have used my eyes well? I fear not having used my time well.

That is the gist of my question. Your time, not only your eyes.

Look, I met you in person only about an hour ago, though I am familiar with your photos and I remember a few things that I have been told about you. If I had to express the idea that I have of you, in a single sentence, I would say "He lives out of a sleeping bag." That would sum up your way of using your time, which is different from mine, and probably more efficient. It's

not that I am dissatisfied with my own life. But I know that too often I have done things that didn't really interest me, or that distracted me from what I thought was my real purpose, because I forced myself to respond to the ideas or the desires of others. I believe that if I was allowed to move back and to relive some hours of my life, the moments I would choose would be those when I was photographing for myself, in the streets of New York or in India. Or even some moments in the studio, when making portraits.

Personally, I have had the good fortune of always being able to do what I wanted, never working for others. Maybe it is a silly principle, but the idea that no one can buy me is important for me. I refuse assignments, even for projects that I have decided to do anyhow. It is somewhat the same with my books. When my first book, the one on the gypsies, was published, it was hard for me to accept the idea that I could no longer choose the people to whom I would show my photos, that any one could buy them.

What are your points of reference – I mean in literature, in painting, in music?

There are a few things that I like very much, but that I do not practice. I have always played music, and I would like to listen to it more than I do, but I don't have the opportunity, due to the lack of time and place. When I was a kid, I did a lot of reading, then a little less during my studies, and hardly any since I left Czechoslovakia – always for the same reason, because I do not have a place of my own. When I travel, I don't even know where I am going to sleep, I don't think of the place where I will lie down until the moment I roll out my sleeping bag. It's a rule that I've set for myself. Because I told myself that I must be able to sleep anywhere, since sleep is important. In the summer I often sleep outdoors. I stop working when there is no more light, and I start again in the early morning. I do not feel this to be a sacrifice, it would be a sacrifice to live otherwise. As for my points of reference, I don't know what they would be.

But, in the world, what seems important to you?

Questions about the world are difficult for me. I mistrust words. I come from a system where words have no value. I got used to not listening much to what people say. Or rather, I listen to them, but I give less importance to what they say, than to the way in which they say it. When someone declares: "I am a communist", (or a socialist, or an anarchist), that means nothing to me. What counts is what people do.

But what else counts for you? Is it important that your photos be preserved after your death?

It never seemed important to me that my photos be published. It's important that I take them. There were periods where I didn't have money, and I would imagine that someone would come to me and say: "Here is money, you can go do your photography, but you must not show it." I would have accepted right away. On the other hand, if someone had come to me saying: "Here is money to do your photography, but after your death it must be destroyed", I would have refused. Do you understand?

What matters is that the photos exist.

Absolutely. Not that they be published or that people admire me. To be known can even be a nuisance. I don't like to feel like the center of attention. I often travel to a horse market in the north of England, where I know just about everyone. When they see me they ask: "Your book, when does it come out? I will never see it, I will be dead before then." And it may be true, some are dead already. But I can always bring to a son the photo of his father, to an old man the photo of when he was not so old. What counts is that the work exists. Besides, I am not someone who likes his own photos very much.

But I have been told that you put them on the wall to see if you can live with them.

I did that in Czechoslovakia, and I would do it again if I had a home. I lived all the time with the photos of the gypsies. If you live all the time with a thing, and you go on looking at it, you end up either by getting tired of it, or by being sure that it satisfies you. For me a good photo is one that I can live with. It's like living with good music or a good person.

Maybe because photography is made essentially of time. I often think that what we show is a point in time, more than a window onto space.

The philosophic aspects of photography don't interest me. What interests me are its limits. I always photograph the same people, the same situations, because I want to know the limits of those people, of those situations, and also my own limits. It's not so important that I succeed in making a photo the first time, nor the fifth, nor the tenth.

I know that when you were photographing the gypsies you often went back to the same places, to the homes of the same families.

I had a specific circuit, where I found the same type of situation again and again. It is what I still try to do, but now it's gotten more complicated. I have neither a car, nor even a driver's license, though I hope to get them. When one works as I do, health problems can become a limitation. Some years ago, I suffered from back pains and the doctor told me: "That comes from your lifestyle." So I took care of myself and recovered, but I know that there will be a time when I will no longer be able to live as I do. When I was thirty, I kept telling myself that at forty a photographer is finished. Possibly this was only to force myself to take advantage of my time. Now I am almost fifty. I still make some good photos and I hope to carry on. But I believe that the truly creative periods are those when you live with intensity. If you lose intensity, you lose everything.

But is it a matter of age? The portraits of women, that I made these last years, are perhaps the project into which I have put the most intensity.

For me, there are few portraits that I truly admire. One time, a funny thing happened: I was near Rome with a pilgrimage of gypsies from Yugoslavia, organized by some Catholic priests. Not actually priests, but some kind of laymen, they earned their living and were nice people. In talking with me, they found out that I was the author of the book about gypsies. They told me that they had a copy of it and that they had cut out the pages, to put them up on the walls of a shack that they used for a chapel. And under each photo the gypsies wrote the name of someone they knew.

They knew the actual people that you had photographed?

No, they knew others, in Yugoslavia, who resembled them. "We know you very well" they said to me, "we call you Iconar". That reminded me of something that I had said to Henri, one of the first times we met, and that made him really laugh: I said that rather than a photographer, I was a collector of photos.

Is that your reason for always going back to the same places?

It's the reason why photography was easier in the beginning. It's like a dart game: at the beginning, you can toss them anywhere, they will always be well placed. Wherever you hit is the right place (in English in the original). But once you start building something, you realize that certain pieces are missing.

So, when you return to those same places, it's with the idea of completing a series, of which some pieces are still missing?

I have a general idea. But as I cannot go everywhere, I limit myself to a few countries in Europe that I feel are close to my way of being: like Spain, Ireland, Italy, Greece. I often return there and I hope to continue returning until I will feel sure of having reached the limits of my possibilities. But I would rather not talk about projects.

Will this work be as important as what you did in Czechoslovakia?

I don't know what's important to the people who look at my photos. What's important to me is to make them. I work all the time, but there are only a few of my photos that I find really good. I am not even sure that I am really a good photographer. I think that anyone working as I do could do the same. But my purpose is not to prove my talent. I photograph almost every day, except when it's too cold for traveling the way I do – as in this time of winter. Sometimes my photos are OK, other times they are not, but I think that eventually something will come out of my work. I don't worry about it. I also take photos of my own life, such as those at the beginning of the small paperback book: of my feet, of my watch. When I am tired I lie down, and if I feel like photographing and there is nobody around me, I photograph my own feet. They are not great photos, some people dislike them. For a similar reason, I always photograph the places where I sleep, and the interiors where I spend some time. It's a rule that I have given to myself, because these are things that one forgets. Maybe one day I'll make a book with them, nothing but those little photos. It may upset some people who know me only as the photographer of gypsies, and who don't want to see me any other way. But I don't care about what people think, I don't try to change people. Nor to change the world.

Second interview, March 1987

You said that you were not very happy with our first interview. I re-read the text, and also I re-read my earlier interviews with other photographers. This made me realize that in the course of these meetings, I partly lost sight of my initial purpose, which was to talk about photography, rather than about photographers. Nonetheless, I would like to begin with a personal comment. I know several people who consider you somehow as their conscience. I know that you are not trying to play the role of guru, but it is your severity toward yourself which leads other people to look at themselves with less indulgence.

You say I am a conscience. That's the last thing I want to be. It sounds as if I judge others, as if I feel superior. I have only been lucky. Because, at the beginning, I was an aeronautical engineer and was able to do photography without the need to be paid. Later, I continued to be lucky, by having the opportunity to work for eighteen years, without having to accept even a single assignment. But this is no reason to make anyone feel at fault, because my way of doing photography is only one among many – and perhaps not even the best.

I would like to see some prints of your work, for example some from the last year, that you said were not quite satisfying to you. And I would like you to explain why.

I don't see any reason for doing that. If I am dissatisfied, it's simply because good photos are few and far between. A good photo is a miracle.

But it may be is easier to explain why a photo is not so good, than to explain why it's good.

But what if almost all are bad? For you, making photos is different, you like to direct. In my case, all depend on what happens, I have to find a situation that interests me. That is why I keep coming back to the same places. But often what I expect doesn't happen, or it happens without my being able to make a good photo.

But what do you mean by "good"?

"Good" is when a situation is at its maximum, and when I myself am at my maximum. It may happen that I reach that maximum the very first time, by chance, and that I return to the place another ten times, over ten years, without being able to do any better. Or that in looking for a certain maximum I find something else, that I hadn't imagined. What matters is my search, my motivation to go further. But I can not sell this way of working to a magazine, I can't expect them to send me ten times to Lourdes, and to have me come back with some photo that has nothing to do with Lourdes!

Was the Prague Spring a maximum? It certainly was an event for which you couldn't prepare yourself and that had little chance of happening again.

It has been the maximum of my life. In ten days, everything that could happen in my life did happen. I was at my own maximum, in a situation at its maximum. That may have been the reason why I "covered" it better than all those professional reporters, who had come from all over the world. I wasn't even a photo journalist. Someone – who in fact knew me rather well – had written about me that I could succeed in any kind of photography, except reportage. Were you aware of it being a maximum, while you were living it? Did you tell yourself every morning: "These days are my maximum, too bad if they cost my life?"

I wasn't thinking about danger. Later, some people who had seen me in front of the tanks said that I could have been killed. But I never thought of that. Even though in ordinary life I am far from brave.

Actually, I was mistaken in saying that you were not prepared: the work that you had done during the ten preceding years had been a kind of preparation. Without that work, you wouldn't have been able to photograph the Prague Spring as you did.

Certainly not. But I do not agree with what that person had written about me. I don't care what people think, I know well enough who I am. But I refuse to become a slave to their ideas. When you stay in the same place for a certain time, people put you in a box and expect you to stay there.

What seems important to me, is that during those days you knew precisely how to see, because you had spent the ten preceding years in training your vision.

I agree with that. But I don't pretend to be an intellectual or a philosopher. I just look.

And you spend your life looking and saying "yes" or "no" to what you see, by releasing or not releasing the shutter, by choosing or not choosing a contact. It is like the binary system of computers, except with many more a "no" than a "yes". What seems interesting to me, are the ten years of "yes" and "no" that prepared you to make, at the moment of the Prague Spring, photographs that others didn't make. Even though the events were the same for all.

Another reason was that I hadn't been parachuted into Prague, like the rest. I was a Czechoslovakian, I was photographing in the country whose language I spoke, whose problems were my own problems. And I was working for myself. Too often people with some talent go where there is some money to be made. They begin to trade a bit of their talent for a bit of money, then a little more, and finally they have nothing left to themselves. In Czechoslovakia we didn't have many freedoms, and particularly not the freedom to make money. But that led us to choose professions that we really loved. I always photographed with the idea that no one would be interested in my photos, that no one would pay me, that if I did something I only did it for myself.

I understand. But what seems the most important to me is what you just said about the maximum. Someone else might have made a few well composed photographs, from behind a tree, and then gone home. You went forward, to search further. Because you had a certain idea of that maximum.

The maximum was in the air. I knew that all the things that could happen in my life were happening. There was a girl I kept running into all the time. At first I was suspicious of her, I imagined KGB spies everywhere. Then that girl approached me, opened her bag and said : "I meet you all the time, you must not have eaten for three days." So I fell in love with her. Everything that could happen did happen. I met all the people whose existence I had imagined. The power of the situation was so great, that it created all those possibilities.

Yes, but if you had not been prepared by the work of the ten preceding years, the situation might have brought you the same intensity, the same love story, but not the same photos.

That comes from my way of working. After having seen my contacts, I do not only print the good photos, but all those that seem to me of some interest, even if I know that they are botched. And I keep looking at them, so as to integrate that experience into my system. Now I can almost photograph without looking through the viewfinder, I have mastered it so well, that it's almost as if I were looking through it. What I want is to find a passage from the unconscious to the conscious. When I photograph, I do not think much. If you looked at my contacts you would ask yourself: "What is this guy doing?" But I keep working with my contacts and with my prints, I look at them all the time. I believe that the result of this work stays in me and at the moment of photographing it comes out, without my thinking of it.

Like a computer program. You spend a lot of time preparing your program, so that at a given moment, in front of a very complex situation, that program permits you to react instantly and correctly.
I would have liked to show you a kind of catalog that I made ten years

ago, where I classified my photos according to their composition. If there is something that you like and that you are interested in, and if, in addition, you have some ability and a little energy to spend, it's bound to work. The program will function. But what is important, afterwards, is to leave the program behind and to move ahead. It would be too easy to let yourself become a prisoner of what you have built, to let the results come out automatically. At some point, one must destroy the program, and start a new one from scratch.

Yes. When I was doing my essay on trees, I realized that as my work was proceeding, my program would get more and more precise, to the point that in the end it became a limitation, making me do the same photographs over and over!

I am not interested in repetition. I don't want to reach the point from where I wouldn't know how to go further. It's good to set limits for oneself, but there comes a moment when we must destroy what we have constructed.

I agree that we should change the program, but I believe that there are some principles that we shouldn't touch.

Which principles?

If only I knew! If I do these interviews, it is precisely to find out. One principle could be to always aim for a maximum, as you say. I know photographers who have given up on that. They do a good job, showing what they choose to show, and what indeed is the representation of some reality, but to me that is not enough.

And why do you think some people give up searching for the maximum?

I only know one answer, which scares me: because they don't have enough energy left.

That scares me, too. We already talked about it in our first meeting, and I told you that the limit could be around forty. It happens to all of us.

On the other hand, Titian made some of his best paintings at eighty. And so did Renoir, Rodin, Picasso. But painting may be a different matter…

Possibly. It's also true that Kertesz made some beautiful photos in his last years – but those were not the kind of photos we are talking about, which demand a certain physical fitness, if only to seek out the situations. It seems to me that in painting there is less difference between a masterpiece and a work that is not altogether a masterpiece. Or at least less difference than in photography: because in painting technique is more important.

Whereas photography depends on the intensity of the moment. I have great admiration for people like Munkasci, who worked with large format cameras, which allowed them to make only one photo in a given situation. He could never give himself a second chance.

You may be right. But I am the product of a different era. If I couldn't shoot lots of photos, I would not be the photographer that I am. Still, the cost of film h as often been a problem. At times, to save money, I had to work with remainders of movie-film, and even to buy film that was stolen. But when I have only three rolls of film left in my bag, I panic.

I understand that. Sometimes I shoot fifteen rolls in two hours, just for a studio portrait. But that does not keep me from feeling that each sitting is a unique event, which can never be repeated.

When I wake up in the morning, and I feel good, I tell myself: "Today may be the last day of my life." That is my sense of urgency. But I keep wondering about what you just said, that I am a conscience. People have told me that. People much younger than myself have told me: "I would like to work as you do."

Only they don't.

Perhaps because they have an idea of me that doesn't correspond to reality. When I left Czechoslovakia, I used to live on milk, bread and potatoes. It became something I was known for. So much that once, at the home of some friends in Holland, whom I was visiting, they put in front of me a plate of potatoes, while they treated themselves to goulash. I don't want to be the slave of my legend!

You refuse to be the slave of money, the slave of your legend... Are you the slave of something?

I am the slave of my mind. I travel alone, I sleep outdoors. Even when I get a lift in someone's car, I separate myself from that person in the morning, and only join up again in the evening. When I arrived in the West, I didn't speak the local languages, so even when I had the money I didn't know how to get served in a restaurant. I'm still unable to write French, I feel like an immigrant worker. I have spent much of my time by myself, with the result that I'm stuck with certain ideas, that may not always fit with reality. I am the slave of these ideas.

But don't you think that the real slavery is the one that we choose? Being a slave to money, as I am, is to some extent the result of a choice. The limits of your mind may be something that you have chosen.

I was born with this mind. It comes from someone who was there before me. But in a certain sense, I chose to be as I am, and it is to this degree that I do not feel it as slavery. It may seem slavery to others, who see me from outside-but for me it's freedom. Which doesn't mean that it couldn't change: now I'm the father of a little girl, and I have to earn money like everyone else. I am fifty years old, it's the time of reckoning. I have done what I wanted, now I have to make good use of the time and energy that are left. Look: all these files contain my contact sheets – which doesn't mean that they contain many good photos, only that I have done a lot of work. It will take years to really look at all that. Even if I fall ill, or if I am immobilized for some other reason, there is plenty of work to be done.

Paris, January and March 1987

Stuart Franklin: stories rarely happen out of the window

Stuart, you studied geography, art and design. What influence does all this have when photo reporting?

Everything influences my work: the things I have studied formally of course; but much more than that, the experiences of living, of life. I started studying painting and drawing. There you learn to take great care in approaching the work. I studied photography. There you learn the techniques, and understand the history of the medium. I studied geography, which is like an octopus. It reaches its tentacles into everything: the land, the sea, the economy, politics, ethnicity, representation, history. So all of this helps me when I am walking around photographing.

When you took the photo of The Tank Man in Tiananmen Square, did you realize that you had an icon on your film, or did the way that the world looked at that picture surprise you?

At the time I felt too far away – on a hotel balcony. I was reminded at every moment of the powerful images from Prague 1968 (so haunting to see today) by Josef Koudelka. And reminded of the saying by Robert Capa: "If your pictures aren't good enough, you are not close enough". So yes I was surprised.

I find that this very image of Tiananmen Square represents one of the rare cases when both the picture and the live TV became icons. What was the strength of that scene?

In a sense, and this viewpoint has been suggested in the book: "No Caption Needed", the single man defying the State became symbolic both of the protest against corruption and lack of free expression in China, but also, conveniently, the photograph became a symbol, an icon, of a Neoliberal ideal – freedom from the State. By this I mean freedom from society, from communal responsibility and so forth. The thinking around this is very interesting.

One year ago you wrote a critical article about Visa pour l'Image. In Perpignan you got the impression that since the war photo reporter cannot solve the conflicts, he can't really make the public aware, so for all these years his role was useless. What do you think is the role of the photo reporter?

I did not have the impression that the war photographer is unable to resolve the conflict. In fact I implied the opposite. The panel of photographers felt, strangely for me, that they had achieved nothing because war still continues. I disagreed. War photography has made a huge impact on policy and public awareness. I felt the photographers who spoke at Perpignan did not give any credit to what they or others had achieved. Don McCullin spoke of shame, when it was his photographs from Biafra that inspired Médecins Sans Frontières to start up in 1971. There are no rules about what people who work with cameras should do: it's their life and time. We hope they will inform us honestly of their experience. That's all.

It is said that photo reporting is like a one-man-show, since he does everything himself. How important is it, also for a freelancer, to have a solid structure that can give him logistical, commercial and even critical support when working?

I have been lucky throughout my career to enjoy the support and encouragement of friends and colleagues. I think we always need people to bounce ideas, to discuss projects, to look at work. Yes this community of support is very important.

In your opinion, style and approach represent the expertise of a photograph. Why?

Style and approach are two different things. Our approach to a story is normally about who we are as an author, as a person. It's about how we will engage with the subject. The style of photography we use (eg large format, colour negative etc), that is a choice often concerned with building a narrative that will be coherent. Within documentary it's a style of visual storytelling that we select.

When you shoot a landscape for your projects of landscape photography, do you have the same approach and style that you adopt for photo journalism?

I have the same approach, because that is who I am – I go gently into the world. The style of working, as I wrote earlier, is quite different.

When you go to a conflict zone, do you plan to follow a story or do you try to cover the news? In your opinion, is it possible for both aims to coexist?

The news is a very multi-faceted thing. It is not necessarily always what is on the TV. A lot of "news" is never reported. Much news is in fact invisible: it was the same in the Great Depression in America in the 30s as in Italy these last years. About unemployment, domestic violence, conflict, things like this. Photojournalists are people who actively hunt for stories, they rarely happen out of the window.

Sarah Moon:
photography provides an
opportunity for staging

an interview by Frank Horvat

Your photos are often criticized as too pretty, as if that prettiness was a formula, an easy way out.

I'm glad you raise the point. It is true that there was this appearance of preciousness, of cuteness, especially at the beginning. I was so seduced by seduction! Now, a whole period of my work seems far away from me, I no longer identify with it.

I didn't mean that I dislike your older photos. Recently I leafed through your books with a group of young people who work with me. We took a sort of poll about the photos we liked most, and often our choice fell on the oldest, for instance the young woman on the path, with the little dog.

It's among the ones that I don't reject.

And the other young woman on a sort of grid, with a little girl who makes a gesture...

"Charlie Girl", I don't reject that one either. It's a black and white photo. I believe that if I didn't work in commercial photography, I would never work in color. It's in black and white that I visualize.

But among our preferences there were also some color photos. The still life with fruits, for example.

The pears. But in that one color is thinned down, manipulated, kind of color without color. That one I like.

Still, you are one of the very few photographers who have found new ways to deal with color.

I don't really like color. To make it work for me, I have to mess with it. I believe that the essence of photography is black and white. Color is but a deviance. Except when one works with very untrue colors, such as Polaroid, or as in certain photos by Paolo Roversi, where color is flattened, so that painting is no longer the reference.

You did, however, find some new solutions, at a time when many people were putting color film into their cameras, while still thinking in black and white (it happened to me) or believing they were doing color photography, when they were only letting themselves be seduced by whatever patch of violent color they found (that happened to me as well, and I'm not proud of it). You increased grain and used it as a kind of filter, to cut out some of the surplus of information recorded by your camera. It's a great idea: as color film carries too much information to be organized into a harmonious whole, you lessen the information by introducing grain, so that you can deal with what's left, in the same way you would deal with black and white.

It's true that grain breaks down colors, like a filter. On the other hand, I am less and less interested in grain for my black and white work, I would rather get sharpness and texture.

Because black and white, by itself, acts like a filter. So grain becomes one filter too many.

Yes, an easy way out.

Besides, some of your black and white photos are perfectly sharp. I think of the young woman, with her back to the camera, wearing a polka dot dress and seated in front of a window. It was another one of our favorites.

Suzanne? Yes, I like that one, too. There are some that I like, of course. But there are many that I now find too cute, that annoy me.

Another issue that seems to preoccupy you is commercial work.

You often insist that working on assignment is not necessarily an obstacle to creativity. I wouldn't dream of contradicting you about this, but I wonder if that is the real problem. For me the problem lies not so much in the assignment, as in the staging. Can a photo be directed, like a movie? Is directing compatible with the essence of photography?

I've always felt that photography provides an opportunity for staging, for telling a story through images. What I aim at, is an image with a minimum of information and markers, that has no reference to a given time or place – but that nevertheless speaks to me, that evokes something which happened just before or may happen just after. I know that many people question this way of photographing, but why should there be only one sort of photography? I want to create images with elements of my choosing, narrative or evocative, beyond the document about that particular woman wearing that dress. I give myself a literary frame, I tell a story. It's the only springboard I have found for taking a leap. On the other hand, I am interested in commercial photography because it provides me with a purpose. The agreement between client and photographer seems perfectly fair to me. They give me the opportunity to make images, on condition that I show their product in a favorable light. I get paid for doing it and am given the means to do it well. This submits me to a discipline, which is something I need, because for me it's easier to do things when I find myself obliged to do them. To do them just for my pleasure would seem irrelevant.

I believe, just as you do, that a photo intended to sell a product can be just as interesting as any other one. But that's not the point that worries me. What I am asking myself is whether a completely staged photo can still be interesting as a photo. Whether there is a threshold, beyond which staging no longer leaves space for the very essence of photography, which is opening a door to the unexpected. For me, this is the greatest problem with assignments. It seems to me that you, in your most successful photographs, allowed for such an opening. And I am sure that when you edit your slides or your contacts, the photo you choose is the one where the unexpected appears.

It is true that when I create a frame, a setting, I always expect that within that frame some accident or some surprise will come up. To seat someone on a chair, for example, can be the beginning of a photo, even though it may not mean much by itself. But if I say, possibly only to communicate with the model: "You sit on this chair, and you are waiting, as if you were on a platform at a railway station," that may introduce the sense of an event, may help me to create the feeling of a situation. Perhaps it is only a device that I need for myself. But now I feel disturbed by what you say, by its expression of reluctance, as if for you the idea of staging is negative, a minus rather than a plus.

Yes and no. If I bring it up, it's not to criticize you, though it is true that I want to pull your strings, just to get your reaction. If only because I had to defend myself on that same issue, facing the criticism of my friends at Magnum, who believed that photography had to be a document and a testimony. For many years they made me feel guilty for not sharing their belief or following their rules.

I used to feel faulted, too, by the "purists" of photography, who saw me as someone who had sold her soul to the devil, because I cashed in my creativity for money. Which they did too, obviously, since they sold their reporting, for less money but with the feeling that they were witnessing some reality. Whereas I only witness my fantasies, my way of seeing beauty in women, which of course is entirely personal, asocial and apparently superficial. Above all, I felt faulted by the little interest that they had for my photos, while I had so much for theirs.

Cartier-Bresson once said to me: "You must choose. It's OK to witness reality, as we do, and it's OK to stage, as Avedon does. But one shouldn't combine the two." I didn't accept this, and possibly I was right, since it is precisely my photos of that period that seem interesting today, and precisely because of that ambiguity. But I would like to return to our starting point: you do still photography, but also film. In both cases, you allow a certain margin for the unexpected. Are the rules of the game identical? Does film allow as much margin? Or is there something different, something specific about the unexpected in a still photograph?

For me it's the same. It's always like a state of grace, like the appearance of something that I hadn't foreseen, that surprises me and stops me. If I only did what I had in mind, there would be no emotion. It would be like keeping one's eyes shut rather than open, like theorizing rather than seeing.

For me a good photo is one that cannot be repeated. I think of, in some of your photos, the hands of those young women and the way those hands relate to each other. "She caught it once" I say to myself while I look at them. "She couldn't ever catch the same thing again."

Because it wasn't planned. When I imagine a situation, I don't imagine the hands. For the one eyed cat with the two girls, what I had imagined was: "There is a sick man, and there are two women caring for him." But the composition, the way in which they move in relation to him and to each other, this I decide later, as I shoot. And in those moments I forget the staged elements. But then: what exactly do you mean by "staging" ? The story? The way of telling it? The directing by the photographer? If what you mean is the directing, then every photo could be considered staged. When you say "don't move!" you direct.

Staging, as I understand it at this moment, is putting in front of the lens what had been in the imagination, as a painter puts outlines and colors on a canvas. If photography is different from painting, it is to the degree to which it depends on the external, and, partly, the unpredictable.

Yes, like a ray of sunlight that makes everything break up, or an underexposure that hides what's in the shadow... I agree. What you call "staging" is what I call "the frame". To begin with, I choose a place, and that already is staging. I say, "I want the light to come through that window and this part of the set to remain in the shade," because I have decided that in my photo it will be seven o'clock in the evening. But my other reason for staging this is to communicate with the models, with the make-up person, with the hair stylist, with all those people working with me.

And also, and this may be the main purpose, because you want

the unexpected to arrive in a precise moment and place. You wouldn't know what to do with an unexpected arriving just anyhow or from anywhere. That wouldn't help you, it would only lead to confusion. So you set limits, create openings, prepare traps where you lay in wait and seize it when it appears.

If it appears. Sometimes it doesn't, or it does but I miss it, or I think it does but I am mistaken. It did appear in the case of the woman with the little dog. That photo was for a calendar, it was to be the last image. I had said to the girl: "It's the time you're going home," so there had been a deliberate staging and directing. But when you look at the photo, you don't think of that, you only feel that something is happening, something that is expressed by her attitude, even though you don't know anything about her. She could be very young or very old, she is without age, timeless.

But all of this could also be imagined by a painter. What a painter couldn't imagine are the effects of light and shadow, the behavior of the dog, the coincidences between these accidents: that's why a photo has be taken at a decisive moment. It all boils down to the decisive moment.

Yes, the moment that might or might not happen. The gift that doesn't depend on us. The best we can do is to be ready – and that's the hardest. All the efforts we invest, the intensity, the waiting, the hoping are not enough. Sometimes we work like mad, for hours, in vain, and then all of a sudden, in three minutes, at the right place, the right moment, from the right angle, a stroke of luck expresses what we wanted to say. In film, this can come through the acting, the editing or the music – in a way it's much easier.

It's another language.

As I'm talking with you, I realize there are many questions about photography that I have never asked myself. Perhaps I keep myself from asking them. At the beginning, there was a sort of drive in my quest, possibly because I didn't know what I was looking for. Then, when my photos began to be accepted, I became aware of certain things, a little as in psychotherapy, where the analyst doesn't give you explicit answers, but refers you back to what you have expressed, and that in turn changes your outlook.

And what did you become aware of?

Of my limitations. Ultimately we keep saying the same thing, even if we try to say it differently. Always the same song. Though in the beginning, I had the impression that each photo was a discovery.

I wonder if it's really the same song. I know that this can be the problem with assignments, and also with success in the media. It's success that keeps us singing the same song, the one they keep asking for. But is it really your only song? There may be other ones…

I believe so, too. But I don't know where they are. If I knew, I would sing them. Sometimes I believe that I hear a note …

There is another sensitive point I would like to touch. One of the leaders in our poll was the photo of the little girl in the street, who appears to spin in a ray of light. We noticed it in one of the catalogues. However, in "Little Red Riding Hood" of which it is part, that photo didn't particularly strike me. Perhaps because I don't care so much for this little book…

What is it you do not like about it?

The very fact of the sequence. I cannot look at the sequence without imagining Sarah staging it – so there is no mystery left. Whereas in front of the single photo I wonder: "Who is this little girl? How did Sarah meet her? What happened?"

It is true that from all these narrative series, intended to appear on three of four magazine spreads, I only show one image in my exhibitions or my books. As if I had only worked for that photo. What bothers you about a series? Is it the variation on a theme?

It's that it takes us backstage.

And possibly the fact that I tell a story with a beginning and an end, instead of letting each image, by itself, suggest a beginning and an end. Repetition gives a key, and with that key, one no longer feels the same curiosity. I agree with that. Very often I say to myself: "I would like to make a photo where nothing happens." My dream would be to achieve that purity. But in order to eliminate, there must be something there to begin with. For nothing to happen, something has to happen first. When I work on a set, with a lot of props, I end up by throwing most of them out, or by mixing them up, or by using mirrors so that one doesn't know what is part of the set and what isn't. I would like to get rid of all the make-up, so that the make-up would be forgotten, to take off all the clothes. I spend my time eliminating things, with the hope that there will be something left that will surprise me, that will make me forget that I am in a studio, in front of a model that I have booked, on a set on which I have spent hours fussing, with lights that it has taken a whole day to set up. Ultimately, what makes me press the shutter is a feeling of recognition. As if suddenly I felt: "yes, that's it ". In fact, these are the very words that come to my lips. I "recognize" something that I had never seen until that moment, that is beyond all my intentions. As in that photo of the polka-dot dress, with Suzanne's back. What I like about it is its weight. It was a moment when I was photographing something else. Suddenly I turned around and there it was. That's what I mean by "a gift".

I have been told – or did you say it? – that you are extremely near-sighted.

As a mole! that's why I have to work with a tripod. But it helps for sensing the light, and also for judging the relations between shapes. I'm good at both. It was only when I started photography that I became aware of it. People would say to me: "But it's not sharp!", and I didn't understand, because that was the way I saw things, I had never worn glasses in my life.

How do you edit your slides? On a projector?

Simply on a light table, with a loupe. You know, I make the same photo two thousand times, over and over, expecting it to happen, being afraid of missing it. I only stop when the people who work for me refuse to continue. And even then I have regrets, I keep telling myself that something else might yet happen.

It's the same for me. What I find astonishing, is that I tend to shoot more and more, while at the same time leaving less and less room for the unexpected. When I photograph in the street,

on the contrary, where millions of things happen all the time, I don't take that many shots or insist on a given situation. While in my studio, with a light that I know well, in front of a model that I have directed into an attitude I find acceptable – and from which I only allow her to try some slight variations, like turning her head or moving her fingers – I could go on shooting ten rolls: because I expect something from those fingers.

Me too. I am there, in front of her, having no idea of what she should do, and even if I had one, not knowing how to tell her. I feel that it has to come from her, it's like hypnotism, I look and look and wait. Of course, from time to time, I click the shutter, if only to encourage her, to encourage myself, to encourage everyone around.

But do you know when you've got the photo? Or are you never quite sure?

Sometimes I know. But most of the time, even when I believe I've got it, I can't stop myself from searching further and soon I forget that I thought I got it.

It's exactly the same for me.

Because it happens so fast. And a second later I'm not sure any more that it has happened. At a given moment, I tell everyone: "That's it, we have finished!" but then I ask them to stay for one more roll, just in case, and then for another one. Because I am always afraid of having missed something, in spite of all the trouble I took to bring together all those elements, which tomorrow won't be there. The passing of time makes me panic. When I feel moved by the beauty of a young woman, what overwhelms me is the impermanence, the feeling that it must be captured in that particular instant. I see beauty appearing and disappearing, and I feel disheartened, because I am never sure that I live up to the privilege, that I do what has to be done to convey what I saw. Our anguish, our feeling of guilt stems from the knowledge that it depends on us, on our way of seeing what's in front of our eyes. Not only that particular sitting seems too short, not only that working day, but our whole life as photographers, we are always afraid that it may already be over. Maybe I shouldn't go too long without working, my engine should run every day, because when it doesn't, I don't give myself a chance to make things happen. I should accept the risk of failure, tell myself that failure is not the worst: even though I can't afford failing an assignment, I have at least the right to fail what I do for myself. I should simply say to myself: "Every day I'm going to make a photo."

Frank Horvat:
photography must catch
unrepeatable moments

Frank Horvat, I recently saw one of your exhibitions and had the impression that at this time in your life you feel very comfortable, and that your work is in constant evolution...

I'm interested in time and in history. And I wish to understand what is going on in the world.

Some photographers seem to stop at their peak...

Yes. A good example is Robert Doisneau, who in the span of about ten years has done some extraordinary work. Then, for him as for others, photography remained what it had been when he was in his twenties or thirties. Many photographers tend to be critical of what is new and to consider contemporary work weaker than past work.

Now many of them believe that in the past every click was premeditated, intentional and perfect, while presently people shoot without much thinking.

For me, it's the opposite: in the past I used to shoot more, simply because I never knew if I had a good shot. So I went on searching. Now I look at my camera screen, and when it seems to me that I got it, I stop. Possibly, my results were better before : because I didn't know what I had, and kept trying.

Anyhow, you seem comfortable with digital photography. Your App for a tablet is quite complex...

Almost too complex. For every image there are several keywords leading to other images. Only these keywords are not simple categories, such as men, women, dogs and cats – but something like viewpoints. The spectator can follow thousands of different itineraries, everyone can follow his own logic. My app works like my brain, by associating ideas. You can start from one image, for instance a family picture, and end up at what I call the human condition. It's a mental trip.

There are also your comments. What do they add to the images?

They help linking the images to each other. I believe that explaining a photo is boring, while it may be interesting to encourage the spectator to associate images and to discover connections between them.

Do you communicate on social medias?

I often find them boring. Their system based on "likes" and "dislikes" seems a bit silly. I find it superficial to judge something without knowing much about it. Just as when people vote without knowing what they are voting for. They can't help reacting emotionally and nostalgically. Or they need to know where and when a picture was taken, in order to connect to some preconceived idea. That's why, in my exhibition in Seravezza, I organized my photos according to keywords. So people have an idea of what to look for, and when they find it they feel that they have been smart, and enjoy that feeling.

When in an exhibition or in a magazine you see one of your photos taken many years earlier, for some advertising purpose, do you feel comfortable with it?

Why not? What is most interesting about a photo is what is left, after all the reasons for taking it are gone.

What are you presently working on?

There are several projects I need to finish, because I'm aware that my time is limited. One is a new app for tablets, that will not be a substitute for my present one, but a presentation of ten year's work with a compact digital camera. I shall call it : An Eye at the Fingertips. What I wish to say is: "Here is what anyone could do with a compact camera (or even with an i-phone)". The focus will not be so much on the single images, as on the passage from one image to the others. In this application, I will show photos that anyone could take. Except that the project should look like something that no one else could have done. The photos will not only speak by themselves, but also by the way they are linked.

Usually it isn't very interesting to talk about technology, tools and cameras, but in your case it really is...

In my life as a professional photographer, the first camera I really felt at ease with was the Leica. Then I discovered the 35 mm reflex cameras. They are different from the Leica, because they allow to see the depth of focus. This encouraged me to take pictures with very poor light. I rarely used larger formats. In New York, where I did an important project, over more than six years, I worked with just one lens, the 85mm. So that I only photographed what that lens was suited for, and I never did any of the classic wide-angle photos of New York. Then, in 1999 – the last year of the millennium – I undertook a year-long photographic diary, all around Europe, with a tiny Olympus camera, and without ever knowing in advance what I would find. I always had my camera in my pocket. Bystanders took me for an old amateur, who was just playing around and couldn't be taken very seriously. A few years later I tried the first Nikon digital cameras, which were huge and heavy. Now I work again with compacts. In fact, they are not as easy to use as you would imagine: because you have to select the right setting. Though sometimes a mistake can produce interesting results....

There are many computers in your studio, do you use them in postproduction?

I'm interested in color, I rarely transform my original color into black and white. But postproduction allows me to enhance what interested me when shooting.

How do you select the pictures?

At this point, I'm not always sure of what I'm looking for: as if some instinct was telling me that a certain situation, in a certain light, could work. And the same instinct tells me which ones to discard.

Do you have a precise project in mind before shooting?

If I had one, I wouldn't even feel the need to shoot. On the contrary, I sometimes shoot to find out what I'm looking for. Henri Cartier-Bresson had this lifelong project to travel around the world, to bear witness about what to him seemed important. But even when his subjects were as important as Gandhi or the Chinese revolution, he didn't press the button unless he saw what to him seemed the right composition. Doisneau didn't worry so much about composition, he wanted to present a certain kind of reality, that made him feel good. Once he told me that his main motivation, for taking photos was to prove that nice people really existed. My own Eye at the Fingertips only became a real project when I began assembling it.

Today, when do you understand that a picture is important?

I don't really know what today is important, but I think that it's important to show how confused and many-sided the world has become. In the thirties, Cartier-Bresson knew that Matisse was important, so he took a great photo of Matisse. He knew that Giacometti was important, and he took a great photo of Giacometti. He knew that China was important, so he went to China and took some great photos. Now everything is multi-faced and mixed-up, and I keep trying to make sense of it. Our age is all at once playful, superficial and tragic. If few of our contemporaries seem to be aware of this, it's because few have any notion of history.

Maybe projects representing our time should also be disorganized and incoherent. A year ago, the photographer Mario Sorrenti came up with his biographic book. His layout is very articulated, but with no clear order, a really complex project.

To me, my layouts and my structures are just as important as my photos, or even more. It's like writing a novel. Structuring an exhibition, an app, a book seems just as essential as shooting. For others, like my friend Boubat, the only decisive moment was the shooting – but then what he got was often extraordinary!

You build paths using keywords. Are the titles of your photos just as important?

In my exhibition in Seravezza the titles were important. The spectator needs a starting point, such as a place and a date, from where he can move to find other meanings.

Why did you shoot so many self-portraits in the many different phases of your life?

Often I take a shot because I'm surprised by what I see. And I'm often surprised when seeing myself in a mirror, or when looking at some part of my body. Another reason is that I am a convenient subject, docile and always available.

Even in the studio and doing fashion photos you manage to find surprises ?

It's harder. That's why I began by shooting fashion in the streets. But later, to make things a little more difficult for myself, I started looking for surprises in the studio. With less and less accessories and props. Then I went as far as to avoid showing the mqdel's face. Because I realised that what matters is not so much what the spectator sees, as what he imagines.

And at a certain point you decided to stop working with magazines?

Maybe they decided to stop working with me.

Do you work a lot with galleries?

They sell my prints.. But most of the time they sell the same photos. Collectors seem more interested in what they already know.

Do people know how to read images?

In general, those who visit a photographic exhibition are interested in photography. I try to help them by providing titles and keys. But this doesn't guarantee that everyone will understand my work. I tend to believe that photography is more difficult to understand than painting and music.

Why do photographers like to shoot in places where there are problems – such as wars?

I believe that many photographers are really concerned with those problems. We all know that we must die, so we are interested in seeing how people die. When some accident happens, people gather and watch, and I don't blame them: they feel concerned because they know that it could happen to them.

Do you think that photography always catches unrepeatable moments?

I think that should catch unrepeatable moments, or at least make us believe that they are unrepeatable.

Massimo Vitali:
I want to see what people are up to

Massimo Vitali, you are known for your large-scale images of beaches, but you actually started as a photojournalist.

Let's say that I'm a reformed photojournalist. My pictures of that period are kept in a closet, and I don't want to see them ever again. I started taking pictures during high school, and then I switched from photojournalism to cinema, all with mediocre results. At some point in my life I thought it was time to start doing something that really interested me. In my fifties I started photography for real and in the last twenty years I developed a coherent path in contemporary art.

At fifty years old did you just decide to start working in contemporary art?

No, if someone thinks, now I want to start making contemporary art, they are already wrong. You need to go with the flow. I was lucky enough to take photography seriously in a moment when major changes were happening in this world.

In the middle of the nineties, you were able to catch a particular moment of the relationship between photography and contemporary art.

Everything was far more accidental than it looks. Trying to achieve any of that in a more organized way, rather than leaving it to chance, would actually be more difficult. I was lucky enough to work on my projects in a moment of transition for photography.

The pictures of the beaches, they came by chance too?

I started shooting at the beach by chance. I took the first beach picture at Marina di Pietrasanta, because I needed to try a tripod that I built with a friend and a new 20×25 camera. So, I just took this equipment to the beach. This was back in 1994, when Silvio Berlusconi had just won the elections and, to be honest, I was very interested by the people that were at the beach.

I read in an interview that you took the first beach pictures because you wanted to see the faces of the people that voted for Berlusconi.

That's right. I wanted to see the people's faces, which interested me a lot. I have a genuine interest towards the people I shoot.

Those who imitate you seem more interested in your visual style, though.

It is quite flattering to be imitated. But whoever shoots "Vitali's way" doesn't necessarily understand what I'm about. All they do is copy the style, the lack of shades and contrasts, the clear colors.
I shoot roughly five meters from the subject, and that's not accidental: I don't use a helicopter or a drone. I want to see what people are up to; I want to feel them. For instance, I'm not interested in the geography of the place.

Does the collector want to know where you took the picture?

Unfortunately, yes. Every time I try to tell them that it doesn't matter where I took that picture: what matters are the details and to try to imagine what the person wearing red shorts is thinking. Of course, in my pictures the sea has a certain color, the beaches are whiter than usual, but at the end of the day, what really matters is the relationship with the people.

Here, there is a contradiction that I believe is crucial in your work. The critics say that your beaches make the people anonymous.

I don't agree with that: for me they are not anonymous at all. Some of my wiser collectors tell me that they establish a mental connection with some of the people pictured in my photos. The figure out stories, they become friends.

But the subjects in the centre of the pictures don't know they are being photographed.

They usually don't. Also, because today being photographed is seen as normal, we got so used to it.

Shooting is only the last step of your work; all your research comes before.

Photography is twenty per cent the image, twenty per cent the print. The rest is assembly and choosing a frame.

That makes sixty per cent marketing.

I don't sell an image. My pictures are on the Internet and as far as I'm concerned, anyone can download them. I sell a piece of art that weighs forty kilos, an object that can be hanged on a wall.

You are very open about that.

I certainly am. At the beginning, I did an exposition with a gallery owner; I had six pictures in total. I told him about my future projects, the other pictures that I had in mind. He told me that I didn't understand anything, and from that moment on all I had to do was to travel the world with these same six pictures. He was absolutely right. At the big international and contemporary art and photography fairs, you see thousands of things hanging on the wall: the essential thing is to be recognized. After two years, even if they did not know my name, they instantly recognized me as that beach photographer.

You started selling photos at a time when art dealers insisted on numbering and having special editions of each piece, something that didn't have anything to do with photography before.

That's right. People can freely access my pictures on the Internet;

they can see it, download it and share it. But when I enter the game of contemporary art, I do accept the exceptionality of the actual, physical object.

Another taboo you are destroying, you are clearly stating that your pictures are beautiful and they are worth hanging on a wall.

When photography started, it suffered from this enormous inferiority complex next to painted art. For such a long time photography took its inspiration from rules that were inadequate for the 1880's, let alone today. Photography managed to free itself when it got rid of the rules of art pompier at the end of the past century and started to use the rules of contemporary art instead.

You are often quoted along with Andreas Gursky, and not only for a simple matter of large-sized prints. I think what you two have in common is the urge to represent the truth in a more complex way compared to those that isolate all the single elements using black and white, strong contrasts, depicting a scene with only a few subjects in the foreground and the rest in the background.

Sure. I have to say one of the biggest inventions of German photographers was that the photos could be taken from a distance. For a portrait, I don't need to shoot ten centimetres from the face; I can be far away, five meters high and obtain a more complex and stratified picture. This genre of far away photography is complicated, contradictory and difficult to explain. What I add to it – and that's a really Italian thing to do – is my need to be close to the people I shoot.

Do your collectors, most of which are foreign, recognize your Italian touch?

I was instantly linked to the German school, but without their constrictions and harshness. Take, for example, Gursky's pictures of the Rhein. He took everything away; he is someone that takes things away.

Do you add things?

I only need what's already there.

In your life you have taken 4700 pictures, as many as a journalist takes in a week. Do you drop some of your ideas?

Marketing must serve a purpose. It helped me to use the beach pictures to sell other pictures, other ideas of mine. I'm currently working on a project about the indigenous populations in Central and South America. I can do this today, but had I done it twenty years ago, no one would have cared for it.

Today I like to be put in front of problems that I wouldn't deal with on my own. That's why I'm accepting assignments like, for example, from the New York Times who sent me to Rome to shoot the Pope's Angelus prayer.

After twenty years, what makes one of your pictures immediately recognizable, even if the subjects and the context change?

That is something that the buyer sees. They tell me: we want a Vitali picture.

When you are doing corporate assignments, do they ask you for that even more?

In corporate assignments I always try to add something of what interests me the most. If I shoot for a bathing suit company, some of the people in the picture will have one of my images printed on a suit. I take the picture following the company requests, but I add that personal touch that makes everything more interesting and unique.

Do you know at what point of your path you are now?

Yes, absolutely. I know if I'm with a gallery I shouldn't be with, I know where the mistakes are, why some things sell and others don't. I've got some great galleries that don't sell anything but do excellent expositions, and others that are less interesting but sell a lot. I decided, for example, to stick with some not-so-great galleries that sell a lot.

If you stop selling, will you give up photography?

Absolutely not. If I enjoy doing something, I'll keep on doing it.

Szymon Brodziak: photography is a gateway to imagination

Szymon Brodziak, I just saw your exposition here at the Helmut Newton Foundation in Berlin and it occurred to me that even as a fashion and advertising photographer, you are attracted by nature most of all.

Actually, all the images of nature that you saw in this exposition are part of my recent work. In the last two years I started looking for new locations, more closely related to nature. What fascinates me about nature is that you can never guess where a certain path will lead you, or what will interest you tomorrow.

In the early years you were very much attracted by abandoned places.

At the beginning I used to shoot abandoned places, big industrial spaces, castles and locations that created a contrast with the model's refinement. In such places I could find many details that filled up the picture. Today, when I'm surrounded by nature I realize that my pictures contain fewer details, which gives much more power to the overall image.

"What you see is what you are" is something that you often say. Does this apply to advertising and fashion photography as well?

This is a very important point in my work. I've never made a distinction between commercial assignments and my personal artistic research. Many photographers make this distinction; but when you cultivate a dream, a scene or a vision within you, then you naturally try to bring this very vision into your commercial work, if your budget allows, that is. What was the question again?

Is it possible to remain faithful to "what you see is what you are" also when you shoot for advertising and fashion?

My secret is to put every idea into words, everything that pops into my mind, every scenario, everything. And whenever I have a new assignment I try to make my idea fit into the brief that I receive. When this works, then I'm able to get a picture that perfectly matches my idea.

In fact, I often ask to the photographers how they feel when they put in an exposition a picture that comes from a more complex work, like an editorial or a photo report.

What I learned from Helmut Newton is that any image can be extracted from a more articulate work, yet it must contain a whole story in itself. The first time that I saw his work I realized that he could tell a complete story within a single picture, a story that the observer can then develop. Photography is a gateway to imagination. I think that the best photographers are those that are able to stimulate your imagination within a single picture, and not within a full series.

Do you think that the theatrical dimension in your pictures is a return to the style of Helmut Newton and David Lachapelle after years of photography in more private, less flamboyant locations?

I'm not attracted by real life or reality. What draws me is a world that I can create using my imagination.

And you, with the help of your team, recreate this world.

Yes, and I am really pleased that you mentioned it. The final product is a result of strong teamwork, where each and every single person adds something to the work; without a well-coordinated team it would be impossible to obtain such results.

Do you always work with the same people?

Yes, whenever possible. But it's also very interesting to meet new people, open up new horizons and gain new experiences.

How do you choose your locations?

In my work it's not the people, but the locations that inspire me. In order to obtain information, I normally inspect the locations at least one day before shooting, and that's the minimum. Doing things spontaneously is more fun, but the result is uncertain and the job more stressful. I see a place and immediately I imagine what can happen there. Moreover, I already picture the whole thing it in black and white.

Do you think that your photography can exist without people?

It could be a good experiment. Like I told you at the beginning, I like exploring and experimenting in new ways.

In the photo with the big tree, the woman is almost hidden.

That's right, that's the direction I'm heading towards.

On your website there are many videos.

I invite a cameraman to join me on the set whenever I can, because I find videos to be a nice complement of my work. People are very interested in what leads to a certain picture.

That's right, the question that we have in mind while looking at a picture is: how did he do it?

And the video is also a memory of the job. When I'm shooting, sometimes I'm not aware of my surroundings: later, when I watch the video, I recall all the fun, the stress, the choices and the movements that lead me to take that photo.

Fashion photography is very often sculptural and definitive. Videos make the context more understandable.

June and Helmut Newton made some videos that helped us

understand Helmut's approach to life. And once you understand his approach towards life, you can understand his photography.

How did you meet June Newton?

I got introduced to June four years ago, here in Berlin, during an exposition. I then met her again at her house in Monte Carlo. I had the mock-up of my book with me and I was petrified, since it is known that June always says what she thinks. She said that she liked my photography but she couldn't do anything for me. When the book was published last year I sent it to her, and she decided to invite me to join this great exposition at the Foundation, that also features Frank Horvat and Helmut Newton.

It's a big responsibility for your future works.

It is. I think it's a huge responsibility; I cannot disappoint a person like June, who believed in my work. I'll keep on doing my job in the best way I know how, always trying to develop and move it in the right direction.

John G. Morris:
truth comes before beauty

John G. Morris, you saw the most important images of the 20th century pass through your office. Every image tells a story of people and places; does using a picture out of its context necessarily mean to fake it?

No, using a picture out of its context does not necessarily mean to falsify it. Maybe, the incorrect use of a caption or a description, an improper editing of the picture makes it false.

What's the biggest case of photographic falsification that you came across?

In 1942, an AP photographer artificially created an entire battle scene in North Africa. But LIFE Magazine, for whom I was working at that time, proved that it was completely fake.

Does time also create fakes? Can a picture published two months after it was shot, for example, also assume a completely different meaning?

Actually, pictures get shot and used later very often, when they seem more appropriate according to the agenda. Most of the pictures are shot and archived and used at a later time. Sometimes this can modify and increase their meaning, but this certainly does not mean to falsify them.

Do you think that today there is a difference between images and photography?

Personally, I use both terms indifferently. If what you mean by this is that an image is a photo that has been modified or retouched, I simply don't believe in using Photoshop for photojournalism.

Is photojournalism supposed to simply be a description of reality?

I think that the task of photojournalism is to tell the Story. For example, Robert Capa's pictures of D-Day are the only ones that got saved that day; I personally edited them for the UK edition of LIFE Magazine. Despite being ruined and not at all clear, they don't look abstract to me. They tell the Story perfectly.

A picture, is it beautiful or is it true?

When I look at a picture all I want to know is what the picture wants to tell me, its message: the truth comes before beauty.

www.ingramcontent.com/pod-product-compliance
Lightning Source LLC
Chambersburg PA
CBHW071801170526
45167CB00003B/1118